The Business Owners' Guide to Handling Tax Issues and the IRS

Tips for Avoiding Trouble with the IRS

Vivian D. Hoard

The Business Owners' Guide to Handling Tax Issues and the IRS

Printed by:
90-Minute Books
302 Martinique Drive
Winter Haven, FL 33884
www.90minutebooks.com

Published in the United States of America

Book ID: 160713-256552

ISBN-13: 978-0692699959
ISBN-10: 0692699953

For more information on 90-Minute Books including finding out how you can publish your own lead generating book, visit www.90minutebooks.com or call (863) 318-0464

Here's What's Inside…

The Best Defense is a Good Offense 1

Sometimes, Interaction with
the IRS is Inevitable 15

Options for Handling an IRS Audit
When Negotiations Fizzle Out
with the Examination Division.........................19

What Is the IRS Office of Appeals?
Why Is It Important? 24

Tax Court is Not Like Divorce Court 27

Who Should Represent the Business
in Resolving the IRS Dispute?.......................30

I Didn't File a Tax Court Petition in Time.
Is All Hope Lost? 35

Employment Taxes are the Worst, Especially
for Young, Rapidly Growing Businesses 36

How to Handle Tax Issues and the IRS.........44

Now Business Owners Can Handle IRS
Tax Issues with More Confidence 46

About the Author 48

The Business Owners' Guide to Handling Tax Issues and the IRS!

Nothing strikes fear into the heart of a business owner more than seeing a letter with a Treasury Department return address and opening the envelope to read, "Your return has been selected for audit." Even though you recorded every debit and credit, balanced your checkbook, had an accountant review your bank statements and records, and just know the return has to be right - your normal rational thought process fails you. You envision handcuffs, prison bars, financial disgrace, and ruin. After all, you have seen enough television shows to know that innocent people are sent to prison all the time.

The truth is that the process is really nothing like that. Hopefully this book will strip the mystery from dealings with the Internal Revenue Service (IRS) and reduce your fear of facing the process of resolving a dispute with one of the scariest government agencies on earth.

I hope this book inspires you to learn more about the process and encourages you to interview representatives, to find one who will represent your interests as an advocate before the Internal Revenue Service and in the United States Tax Court.

To Your Success!

Enjoy the book!

Vivian

The Best Defense is a Good Offense

Jonathan: What are the best strategies for a business owner who hopes to avoid problems with the IRS?

Vivian: All I do is handle tax disputes with the Internal Revenue Service ("IRS") so I have had the opportunity to observe the biggest mistakes that get business owners into tax trouble. This book is designed to teach business owners about the worst mistakes so hopefully they can avoid trouble with the IRS in the first place. However, if they have already made mistakes, the second purpose of this book is to give business owners the knowledge to confidently manage problems with the IRS.

Business owners just have to remember to be

S-M-A-R-T.

S- Seek good advisors.

M-Maintain Books and Records.

A-All Returns must be timely filed.

R-Review tax compliance before year-end.

T-Too good to be true? Then it is.

<u>Seek Good Advisors</u>

First, good advice is an important investment. A business owner must hire the right professionals. People never want to spend money for professional services, but it is always less expensive to spend the money at the beginning to structure transactions appropriately to avoid problems than to pay a professional to clean up the mess caused by lack of planning.

Hiring a reputable Certified Public Accountant ("CPA") and attorney are mandatory tasks. Do not skimp on these services.

Anyone can hang a shingle and prepare taxes, so it is important to hire someone who is accountable under the appropriate professional standards. A CPA must have a license and complete mandatory continuing education requirements. In some states, individuals must register as a tax preparer and demonstrate tax proficiency. Enrolled Agents also must adhere to certain professional standards. The business owner should find someone with credentials who knows federal and state tax laws, and can help the client navigate the labyrinth of federal and state tax rules and forms. Tax law is difficult and the rules change periodically. I have observed many situations in which taxpayers have followed the advice of someone with no formal training in tax law, and they get into serious trouble because of it.

Like CPAs, attorneys are also licensed and must complete continuing legal education requirements. It is helpful to have a business attorney with a tax background such as a Master of Laws in Taxation (LLM) or an attorney who is also a CPA. At the very least, a corporate attorney should have substantial tax experience or access to a tax department that can help with tax issues. Frequently, mid-sized to larger firms will have a tax department to assist business lawyers with structuring transactions in compliance with tax laws.

Everything done by a business has a tax consequence, from deciding whether to lease or purchase equipment, whether to structure a transaction with debt or equity, or whether it is more appropriate to expense an item rather than capitalizing and depreciating it.

- These are samples of the kinds of questions that need answers:
- Do I want to be a corporation or partnership?
- What entity is best if I want to go public?
- Does the business want to acquire a competitor?
- Should the taxpayer buy stock or assets?
- How do owners allocate purchase price in an asset purchase?
- Will it allocate any of the purchase price to goodwill?
- Should owners put real estate into an S corporation or into an LLC?
- Can they pay rent to their LLC and also deduct it?
- I want to retire. Would an ESOP be a good idea?

The first thing business owners or principals must decide is which business entity is more advantageous for their particular business. State laws govern the formation and operation of the business entity, but federal tax laws determine how the entity is taxed.

The simplest entity is a sole proprietorship. Income and expense for a sole proprietor are reported on a schedule C of the proprietor's Form 1040 individual tax return.

However, since sole proprietorships do not enjoy limited liability from state law tort claims, most business owners opt for another entity. The choice boils down to a pass-through entity that only taxes income at one level - the owner level - or a C corporation in which the income is taxed at both the corporate level and again at the shareholder level when profits are distributed. To avoid two levels of tax, most people opt for a pass-through entity such as a limited partnership, an LLC, or an S corporation.

It is important to review the basic structures including their pros and cons, given the business entity involved. Review the options with both the CPA and attorney, because CPAs and attorneys frequently have different opinions about the best structure for the business. Both professional types have seen instances in their own practices which have led them to believe that one or the other structure might be better for a particular type of business. For instance, S corporations are limited in the number and type of legally allowed shareholders. This might prompt the advisor to suggest a limited liability company ("LLC") or partnership. There are ways to convert one type of entity to another type. Sometimes the conversion is required because the parties couldn't anticipate the future path of the business, which could lead to tax consequences, so anticipating the needs of the business is a requirement.

Some individually owned businesses might want to form an LLC.

However, the owner may not realize that a single member LLC is a disregarded entity for tax purposes; therefore, the income and expense of the business is reported on a Schedule C of the owner's Form 1040 individual income tax return just like a sole proprietor. The owner will still have liability protection, but research suggests individuals who file a schedule C are audited more frequently than other taxpayers. Therefore, the business might decide to add an entity member to the LLC to avoid single member status. They could also file an election to be treated as a corporation. A C corporation files a Form 1120 tax return. An S corporation files an entity-level information return on a Form 1120S, but the income and expense flow through to the individual shareholders on a Form K-1. To qualify for S corporation status, the entity is required to timely file an election. A partnership files an entity-level information return on a Form 1065, and the income and expense flow through to the partners on a Form K-1. These are just samples of the things a new business owner would learn from their CPA or attorney.

Maintain Books and Records

The second rule that a business owner must follow is to maintain books and records of accounts and transactions. These books and records are required by the Internal Revenue Code ("Code"), and they can come in handy if the business is ever audited. Business owners concentrate on earning money and growing the business, which is understandable, but they cannot ignore the paperwork.

A big problem, particularly in cash-intensive businesses, is the lack of cash controls.

A business needs a process for documenting cash receipts and expenditures in cash. A business owner will need to make sure that their CPA sets up a protocol for cash controls so all cash flow can be traced.

In certain industries, business owners have a tendency to pay workers in cash. That is problematic because a paper trail is important. For instance, perhaps due to cash flow problems, a business pays its workers in cash to avoid paying the employers' share of employment tax, and uses those funds to pay for operations. Besides risking criminal prosecution and delinquent employment tax penalties, the business owner will have problems deducting salaries if those cash salaries cannot be documented.

Owners may have spent their cash, but they won't get a deduction if they can't prove by some documentary evidence that they actually made that payment.

To help maintain the books and records, a growing business might consider hiring an internal bookkeeper. Always enlist the assistance of the CPA to help find a knowledgeable bookkeeper. Hiring a bookkeeper does not mean the business owner can delegate all responsibility and ignore the business's records or tax compliance responsibilities. On the contrary, a business owner who delegates the responsibility of filing returns and paying taxes to that internal bookkeeper will be ultimate responsible for the tax liabilities if anything goes wrong.

According to Martha Stout in her book *The Sociopath Next Door*, around 4% of the population are sociopaths.

They have no conscience. So while the odds are good (96%) that the bookkeeper is honest, the remaining 4% make it important to monitor the activities of the internal bookkeeper at all times.

All Returns Must Be Timely Filed

The third and most important rule is to timely file all returns and pay all taxes. If paying the tax is currently impossible, at least timely file all returns. Managing this one task can save a business from a world of hurt. Late filing and payment penalties cost business owners a dramatic amount each year. The typical entity returns are the annual returns such as these: Forms 1065 for partnerships or LLCs electing partnership status, Forms 1120S for subchapter S corporations, Forms 1120 for C corporations. Forms 941 employment tax returns (and the corresponding information returns), Forms W-2 and 1099, and the Forms 940; as well as the corresponding state tax returns. The penalties for failing to timely file a return will fully accrue much more quickly than the penalties for failure to pay the tax amount itself, so file the return on time even if the business lacks the cash to pay the tax at the time the return is filed.

Unfortunately, many businesses will not timely file their returns if they lack the money to pay the tax. That is a bad idea! Even if the business can't afford to pay the tax immediately, it's important to file the tax returns on time and then work to establish a payment plan with the IRS.

Contrary to popular opinion, most IRS revenue officers will work with business owners of cash-strapped businesses on a payment plan that helps the owners to stay in business so they can continue to employ their workers.

This scenario of non-filing happens routinely in trust fund tax cases. Federal and state employment taxes and state sales taxes are known as "trust fund taxes". When a business withholds employment taxes from the employee and collects state sales tax from a customer, those tax dollars do not belong to them. The business is merely holding those tax dollars in trust for either the federal or state government. Hence, the name of 'trust fund liability' means the business owner is personally liable for payment of those taxes and cannot bankrupt out of that personal liability. Business owners with cash flow problems should never use trust fund taxes to fund operations. Try to get a line of credit instead. I have seen business owners with cash flow problems think they will be able to make up the deficit over a period of time, but they keep falling further and further and further into debt.

Any business owner who falls behind on the business's tax payments needs to meet with an advisor to create a plan for resolving the problem, and set up a payment plan with the IRS in order to minimize penalties. The IRS will work with people who are proactive and refuse to bury their heads in the sand.

Review the State of Tax Compliance Before Year-End

Rule number four is that the business owner should conduct an annual tax review with the business's CPA and attorney prior to the end of the year. This review involves assessing the state of the business, fully documenting any undocumented transactions throughout the year, and ensuring compliance with all of the business tax requirements.

Pay for that hour of time. Again, it is more cost-effective to correct problems earlier rather than later. The CPA should determine if owner partners, LLC members, and/or S corporation shareholders have paid sufficient estimated taxes during the year.

Employees receive a W-2 and the employer pays a portion of the employee's employment tax. Self-employed individuals pay both the employer and workers' share of employment tax as self-employment tax. Owners in partnerships and LLCs will receive distributions, and must pay quarterly estimated tax payments. If they underpay on estimated taxes, they must pay an estimated tax penalty. S corporation shareholders who work in the business will receive both a W-2 and a K-1. Check with the accountant prior to year-end to confirm that sufficient withholding and estimated taxes have been paid.

Too Good to be True? Then It Is

Finally, the fifth rule for every taxpayer is this: if anything seems too good to be true, it probably is.

Congress has enacted certain tax incentives like conservation easements, energy tax credits, and rehabilitation credits, and there are other legitimate tax savings provisions like retirement and profit-sharing plans that can help reduce the tax burden. States have enacted other incentives such as state film tax credits. These types of tax incentives or tax-favored provisions are all legitimate if they are structured appropriately. But too many clients have come to me for help after they have followed the advice of people who have advertised as tax advisors, who are looking out more for their own best interests than the client's best interests.

These individuals will charge taxpayers thousands of dollars to structure tax strategies that either do not exist or do not work.

In one case, the attorney who structured the deal for my clients went to jail, but the taxpayers still had to pay the delinquent taxes plus interest on the tax. Fortunately, the IRS realized that my clients were victimized by this unscrupulous attorney and abated all penalties. The moral of that story is to get a second opinion before engaging in a too-good-to-be-true transaction. Otherwise the taxpayer could be hit with negligence penalties or, God forbid, even fraud penalties. The negligence penalty is 20% of the understatement of tax whereas the fraud penalty is 75%.

Another client was investigated by the Criminal Investigation Division of the IRS for following the incredibly bad advice of a CPA in Texas. When the client hired me for help, I explained the problems with the Texas CPA's advice, so he followed my advice and amended his returns to correct the errors.

Thankfully, when he amended his returns upon learning that the Texas CPA's advice was wrong, the criminal division of the IRS decided not to pursue a prosecution. So remember, if it seems too good to be true, it probably is, so follow up with the long-time tax advisers and attorneys of the business before doing anything that sounds too good to be true.

Jonathan: How much research would be needed for a business owner to be knowledgeable about tax laws and IRS taxes? Is that a requirement for all business owners?

Vivian: Business owners are entitled to rely on the substantive advice of their tax advisors, provided the owners have given their advisors all of the facts of the transaction, and that the tax advisors are competent. Running the business is hard by itself, but as long as the business owners have good advisors they trust, and the owners provide their advisors with the necessary information to make a reasoned decision, they should be protected. Tax law is hard even for tax lawyers and CPAs. Tax law changes as courts interpret the Code and its regulations. In addition, the IRS frequently issues notices regarding changes in various procedures and filing requirements. A good tax lawyer will spend a portion of each day reading the updates or emails sent by his tax research service. Given tax law complexity, it would be unreasonable to hold a taxpayer to the same high standard as his advisors. Taxpayers must exercise ordinary business care and prudence in selecting a competent advisor, and understand the issues well enough to know when they need to ask their tax advisors for help.

While business owners can rely on the substantive advice of their tax advisors they cannot delegate the responsibility of timely filing the returns to their tax advisors. So business owners need to know the various deadlines for tax returns and they need to meet those deadlines.

Jonathan: I want to talk a little bit about the CPA in Texas who gave your client bad advice. How would a business owner determine the legality or legitimacy of a piece of advice? I know you said if it's too good to be true, but what if the owner trusts the CPA enough to believe him?

Vivian: As long as the business owner follows rule number one and has hired a reputable accountant or attorney, the owner should be protected. Of course it is necessary to research the attorney's background and get recommendations for CPAs, and vice versa. Of course there are exceptions like the Son of Boss tax shelter transaction that brought down a reputable law firm, or other tax shelters structured by reputable accounting firms that get too "creative" for their own good. Those situations create problems. Whether penalties are or aren't abated in those instances depends on the sophistication of the taxpayer. Someone running a successful business will have a difficult time getting out of penalties if some tax strategy generates a $50 million dollar loss to shelter a $50 million gain on the sale of the business, but an unsophisticated shareholder who doesn't work in the business and has received the benefits through a flow-through entity might be protected from penalties.

The best advice is either to use a trusted tax advisor with whom the business has a long-term relationship or build a relationship with a tax advisor and get a second opinion if the transaction is too good to be true. Issues occur when the client attends some seminar in a hotel room and the promoter of the transaction starts to say things like, "We know more about this than your accountants in Atlanta. They're just not sophisticated enough to undertake transactions like this." Other situations arise when promoters try to convince taxpayers that they can somehow avoid paying taxes by placing their money offshore. That is not true. United States citizens are taxed on their worldwide income. Don't believe anyone who says differently. Finally, if a business owner thinks his (or her) tax advisors are not sophisticated enough to understand the transaction, and then get a second or even a third opinion. Better to be safe than subject to penalties.

Jonathan: Let's say a business is paying its employees outright with cash. Is that a red flag for the IRS to take action, as if it seems like employees are getting paid underneath the table and the business is trying to avoid tax?

Vivian: Yes. Operating in cash is always a red flag. Sometimes employers will try to hide cash payments to workers in a separate line item on the return, like cost of goods sold. The owner is trying to pay in cash yet still get the deduction. That isn't a good idea. The better idea is to hire documented workers and pay them by check so the business can verify the payment. If the business is audited, the burden of proof will be on the owner to prove expenses, and it's difficult to prove expenses without a paper trail. Checks are wonderful because they provide a paper trail. At the audit, the business just produces the check to prove payment. I doubt that the employee who accepted a cash payment will show up at the audit and admit receipt of the cash payment, especially if the employee did not include the cash payment on his return.

Sometimes, Interaction with the IRS is Inevitable

Jonathan: What happens if a business owner follows your top five rules and gets audited anyway?   What should a business owner expect if the IRS audits?

Vivian: Sometimes a business can be doing everything right and the IRS will still audit. I handled several NFL football player audits a few years ago, because apparently the IRS decided they needed to audit NFL football players. Sometimes the IRS audits a particular industry or a particular transaction. The IRS is currently auditing conservation easements and captive insurance companies, as well as returns showing big losses or a series of substantial losses over a period of years, like the losses reported by Donald Trump that became an issue during the 2016 presidential election. Special rules apply to some industries like the real estate industry, and these returns are frequently audited. Sometimes an audit is just the bad luck of the draw.

Being audited can be frightening but it is more of a nuisance than anything else. There are strategies for managing the audit and trying to reduce the heartburn. Any business owner selected for an audit should remember that it is just business; an audit is nothing personal, so do not make it a personal matter. Do not be confrontational, sarcastic, obnoxious, or defensive. Do not turn into a sycophant either. Be professional, courteous, and brief. In fact, it is best to have the business's accountant handle the audit to prevent personality conflicts which could escalate the audit.

There are several types of IRS audits, although all audits are conducted by the Examination Division of the IRS. The most dreaded and most mimicked type shown on television is the in-person audit; the auditor will go to the taxpayer's business and review the business returns, and sometimes the owner's individual returns, line by line. Typically, the IRS Revenue Agent (also called an auditor) will do a bank deposit analysis. That means the auditor will compare the bank deposits of the business with the cash showing on the return to ensure that all cash is reported. The auditor will also compare wage and income reports such as Forms 1099 or W-2s against the individual taxpayer's return to ensure that all items of income have been reported. If there is a discrepancy, the taxpayer must prove that certain deposits are not income, as for example, a loan deposit. This is where good record keeping comes in handy. Next, the auditor will generally spot-check the expenses on the return to confirm substantiation for the expense. If the taxpayer can substantiate the expense with the appropriate records, the agent will conclude the audit much earlier. Substantiating income and expense requires more than the entries in QuickBooks. Substantiation requires the taxpayer to produce the source document such as an invoice or check. Computer records in QuickBooks could be easily altered, so the IRS will want to see the source documents.

Another type of audit is a correspondence audit. The IRS has several computer programs that match wage and income reports provided by the payer to the IRS, linked to the taxpayer's tax identification number. The IRS will match those reports against the taxpayer's return.

Sometimes individuals will miss a W-2 from a temporary job or the Form 1099 for a particular investment. The taxpayer must present evidence that the income on the Form is not income or that it was already included on the return yet on a different schedule. Many times, the items have been listed on a different line on the return than an expected area, so if the taxpayer can prove the amount was on the return, the audit should conclude rather quickly.

Certain types of issues are considered high-profile and it is more difficult to make these types of cases go away. These include conservation easements, captive insurance companies, and some family limited partnerships. Passive loss issues are also frequently audited, invoking the material participation rules. Many of these issues are fact-intensive and sometimes an auditor will not be able to resolve the case. The tax code is not black and white. It is gray, and in a gray area an auditor may feel a decision is above his paygrade. If his supervisor agrees, the business owner may hear the auditor say: "I am not going to agree with you. I am writing up the case in accordance with my interpretation of the Internal Revenue Code and Mr. Taxpayer, you can either agree or take it up with the Office of Appeals or the United States Tax Court."

When that happens, business owners tend to panic and waste a lot of money because they are afraid of what will happen next, generally the case will go to the Office of Appeals or the United States Tax Court.

The taxpayer will often want me or their accountant to make one more attempts at settlement with the supervisor, but once an auditor and his supervisor make up their minds, it is rare for the taxpayer or his counsel to change their mindset. But business owners will waste money trying. Many times the auditor has been told by the supervisor, "Close the case." The supervisor wants the audit out of his inventory. Taxpayers get nervous when that happens and for some reason, believe the IRS has it in for them. But remember it is not personal. For the IRS agent, these actions are just part of the job. It is just one more case in his inventory to close. One of my associates had previously worked with a firm that would repeatedly butt heads with the IRS auditor and rack up large fees. He was amazed to later learn that "litigation" can often be much less expensive than some extended audits.

One of the purposes of this book is to calm taxpayers' fears when they cannot resolve the case at the audit level.

Options for Handling an IRS Audit When Negotiations Fizzle Out with the Examination Division

Jonathan: So what is the next step?

Vivian: The next step will be to take the case either to the Internal Revenue Service Office of Appeals or to the United States Tax Court. The Tax Court case will be sent back to the IRS Office of Appeals for possible settlement before trial. Everything leads back to this Office of Appeals.

At the end of the audit, the auditor will write what is known as a Revenue Agent's Report that outlines the various issues with the return and proposes certain adjustments to the return. The taxpayer will then receive either a "30-day letter" or a "90-day letter." The 90-day letter is also known as a Statutory Notice of Deficiency (SNOD). To understand which one of these letters the taxpayer will receive requires an understanding of the statute of limitations in a tax case. Generally, the IRS has three years to propose adjustments to a return. The time is extended to six years if there is a 25% understatement of income. If the IRS believes the taxpayer engaged in fraud, the IRS can argue that the statute never expires and can propose adjustments to the return at any time.

If the IRS does not act within the time limits, then they are barred by the statute of limitations from making any adjustments to the taxpayer's return. The next move in the case depends upon the statute of limitations.

The Office of Appeals requires a year to be remaining on the statute of limitations before they will receive a case at the conclusion of the audit. That means the taxpayer may have to extend the statute of limitations if she wants to go to Appeals directly without paying the $60 filing fee to file a Tax Court Petition and then go to Appeals

My mantra is that nothing gets better with age. In only a few instances would I recommend that anyone sign an extension of the statute of limitations. Many clients are afraid not to sign the extension and even some CPAs will say, "If I don't sign, the IRS won't like me." Some taxpayers believe they will make the IRS mad if they don't sign. Taxpayers have a right to a speedy resolution of their tax dispute and they are not required to extend the statute of limitations. If I'm dealing with the IRS, they know that in general I will not sign an extension of the statute and they know it's nothing personal.

Taxpayers have to do things timely, so it is not unreasonable to ask the IRS to be timely as well. They do not get angry just because a taxpayer will not sign an extension of the statute of limitation. I've seen situations in which people lose records or witnesses die while the case is under extension. The taxpayer has the burden of proof and unfortunately, some of the taxpayer's evidence may disappear over time. It is better to deal with the case while things are fresh in everyone's memory, before the paper has disintegrated, or before the computer's hard drive has crashed. We all have a tendency to procrastinate. We want to put things off because we do not want to deal with it today but it's not good to put it off. Just deal with it.

If plenty of time is left on the statute of limitations, the taxpayer can go directly to the Office of Appeals ("Appeals"). To get to Appeals, the taxpayer files a Protest of the Proposed Adjustments explaining the evidence that supports the position taken on the return and the legal authority that supports that position. The Office of Appeals has recently changed its procedures and generally requires a year on the statute of limitations before taking a case directly from the examination division. Because of the new rules, very seldom will a case with a three-year statute first get sent to Appeals without an extension. In that situation, the auditor will tell the business that it can't go to Appeals if the principals do not sign the extension. The auditor will tell the taxpayer that he (or she) must go to Tax Court instead. That statement about procedure is misleading. If the taxpayer does not sign the extension, she will receive a Statutory Notice of Deficiency (SNOD). Once the taxpayer receives the SNOD, she files a Tax Court Petition and pays a $60 dollar filing fee. The government files an answer within 60 days, and then the case is sent back to Appeals for possible resolution.

The Office of Appeal is a wonderful thing in the IRS; the Appeals Officers are required to be independent, which was the whole purpose of this office. The government realized that sometimes people are sensitive. They don't want the IRS telling them they did something wrong, and the IRS employees don't want taxpayers claiming they're doing something wrong. So personality conflicts can arise.

Someone neutral is better able to help resolve the case.

For the most part, the Appeals Officers are neutral; provided the taxpayer has provided them with all of the information they need to make a decision, taxpayers can reach an acceptable resolution with the Appeals Officer. Occasionally, there are times when the Appeals Officer doesn't feel like he can resolve the case. When that happens, the taxpayer must negotiate with the IRS attorney for a possible resolution. Just because the case isn't resolved in Appeals, doesn't mean the IRS attorney won't resolve the case prior to trial. The IRS attorney has the final say in deciding whether or not the case is a good case to try. These attorneys have trial experience and have handled many of the same issues over and over again; they know what the Tax Court decisions say, and have a better feel for how the Tax Court will rule. They can sometimes make a decision that nobody else is willing to make.

The good thing about the folks at the IRS, particularly the attorneys, is that they are just looking for the right answer. They do not try cases to run up their fees. They want to figure out the right answer based on the particular facts of the case at issue. Also, I have found IRS attorneys to be pleasant and professional; again, the issue is not personal. Tax Court doesn't work in the same way as Divorce Court, in which some attorneys during the divorce case don't want the case to settle because they make more money by keeping the controversy going.

The Tax Court is called "the people's court" because it is people-friendly. That does not mean it is informal.

It is still a formal court, scary to every litigant, but the judges are cognizant of taxpayer rights. They want to make sure the taxpayers have their say in court and are treated fairly.

What Is the IRS Office of Appeals? Why Is It Important?

Jonathan: You keep saying IRS Office of Appeals. What exactly IS the IRS Office of Appeals?

Vivian: The Office of Appeals is a group of individuals within the Internal Revenue Service whose job is to solve tax controversies without litigation. In fact, the Code says the mission of the Appeals Office is to resolve tax controversies without litigation on a fair and impartial basis to both the government and the taxpayer, in a manner that will enhance voluntary compliance and public confidence in the integrity and efficiency of the IRS.

The Appeals Office serves as a mediator between the taxpayer and the IRS. They take a fresh look at the case. They listen to the taxpayer's concerns. They listen to the taxpayer's version of the facts, review the legal authority provided by the taxpayer's attorney, and try to resolve the case. They are a good option to have when the taxpayer and the auditor have stalled because of a personality conflict or a genuine disagreement over the proper tax treatment of an item. The Appeals Officer brings a fresh set of eyes to the case.

Appeals Officers recognize that the law is gray, and sometimes there is no clear answer on point for a particular set of facts. Therefore, Appeals has been given a lot of flexibility to settle cases. For instance, let's say the taxpayer has some good reasons why they don't owe the tax, but the IRS has come up with some reasons why they think the taxpayer owes the tax.

The Appeals Officer can consider hazards of litigation, and has the option of crafting a Hazards of Litigation Settlement to resolve the issue. For instance, the Appeals Officer may believe that the taxpayer has a 75% chance of prevailing and may be willing to offer a 75% settlement in the taxpayer's favor to avoid the 25% chance of losing the case. This type of settlement is comforting to taxpayers, since no one can predict the outcome of the trial when the case involves a gray area.

Jonathan: What is the process of appeal?

Vivian: I know people get confused when they hear the word "appeal." Most people think an appeal comes after the trial of a case. The name of the Office of Appeals can get confusing, but every procedure within the IRS leads to the Office of Appeals. Previously, I mentioned petitioning a case to the United States Tax Court. The case will go back to Appeals for possible settlement before the case is actually tried. District Court is another venue where taxpayers can challenge an IRS assessment, but they have to pay the tax first. Even in District Court cases, the matter will first return to Appeals for an attempt at resolution of the case. When a taxpayer owes a tax but cannot pay, the IRS must allow an opportunity for the taxpayer to have his case heard in Appeals before the IRS can levy on the taxpayer's assets. If a spouse signs a joint return, each party is jointly and severally liable with the other spouse. An innocent spouse may seek to be relieved of the liability by filing an Innocent Spouse Request. If the request is denied, the spouse can seek to have Appeals review the case before filing a Tax Court Petition.

An appeal is a wonderful way to try to solve a dispute with the IRS prior to trial.

Jonathan: So, everything essentially works its way through the Appeals Office; from there, it's IRS and then ultimately to court?

Vivian: A taxpayer can be heard in three courts. A taxpayer can file in Tax Court prior to paying the tax if the case is filed timely. After the taxpayer pays the tax, and provided the taxpayer didn't file in Tax Court, a taxpayer can either seek a refund in District Court serving the district where the taxpayer resides or does business, or in the Federal Court of Claims in Washington, D.C. If the case goes to the Tax Court, IRS Counsel will try the case. If it goes to District Court or the Court of Claims, a Justice Department Tax Division Attorney will try the case for the government. District Court and the Court of Claims are more expensive than Tax Court. Those cases operate more like a divorce case involving numerous and expensive depositions and reams of paper discovery. The filing fee is also much higher. The difference in cost is the reason why most taxpayers choose Tax Court.

Tax Court is Not Like Divorce Court

Jonathan: Whether it's Tax Court or whether it's a District court, I don't want to go to any court. Isn't any court expensive?

Vivian: If you have to litigate a tax case, Tax Court is the least expensive option. As I said, Tax Court is not like a divorce court. Tax Court is civilized. The attorneys are reputable and generally work together to get the right answer and it only costs $60 to file the petition.

Jonathan: Wow.

Vivian: The Tax Court judges sit in Washington D.C. but trials are scheduled all over the United States. In my home state of Georgia, the Tax Court hears cases several times a year in Atlanta. I have handled cases for taxpayers all over the Country but if the taxpayer agrees, I can file the Petition and designate the trial to be held in Atlanta, Georgia. The 'law of the circuit' where the taxpayer resides will still apply to the case, but it can cost much less if the lawyer does not have to travel.

The tax attorneys who represent taxpayers in Tax Court are dealing with a group of IRS attorneys they deal with frequently. Both sides see the same substantive issues come up over and over again, from passive loss cases to real estate professional cases. They will have had a conservation easement case with the same issues as the one currently before the court. Because they have worked opposite each other for so long, both sides may already know the right answer and be able to resolve the case more efficiently.

Most cases are settled before trial. The types of cases that are more likely to end up in trial involve issues of first impression, meaning that no court has interpreted the particular statute or regulation involved. Factually intensive questions or valuation issues that arise in certain types of cases like conservation easements or family limited partnerships might also be tried, if the parties cannot agree on the facts involved or reach a mutually agreeable compromise. Frequently those cases are settled by Appeals based on hazards of litigation because neither side wants to risk losing.

In Tax Court, a taxpayer can avoid having to take personal depositions and pay for depositions of all the witnesses, besides the tedious and time-consuming expensive discovery process that is followed in most courts. Prior to filing a Petition in Tax Court, the taxpayer should file a Freedom of Information Act Request to the IRS to obtain the government's entire file. That dispenses with the need for extensive interrogatories or requests for production of documents. The taxpayer has the government's entire file. The file is the roadmap to the government's thinking when its officers made a determination.

Furthermore, in most courts, attorneys do not engage in the extensive stipulation process required by the Tax Court rules of practice and procedure. In most trials, the attorneys must go through the tedious process of authenticating each piece of documentary evidence with the repeated litany, "I'm showing you what's been marked petitioner's exhibit number 1 for identification. Do you recognize that?"

Going through that process with thousands of papers during the trial would cost a fortune. In Tax Court, the parties are required to stipulate to all documents to which there can be no reasonable disagreement. When the parties are required to stipulate to most of the evidence, the trial ends up being a day or two days at the most, as compared to District Court where a trial can last for weeks. That saves both time and the hourly rate of the attorneys involved in the case.

Depositions are rare in Tax Court as well. If the parties cannot agree to a deposition of a particular witness, then the party must seek permission to take the witness's deposition from the judge. That seldom happens.

The other positive aspect of trying the case in Tax Court is that the Tax Court judges are tax experts. They're very knowledgeable because all they do is work through tax-related cases.

If the case is tried, the parties stipulate to the documents and introduce any necessary witness testimony to make a record of the case. A court reporter transcribes the testimony. At the conclusion of the case, both parties prepare briefs outlining the facts and the law, and why the law favors their side. A few months after receiving the briefs, the Tax Court will issue a written opinion.

Who Should Represent the Business in Resolving the IRS Dispute?

Jonathan: How would someone, a business owner, find the right attorney for a tax case if it does eventually end up going to Tax Court or, God forbid, District Court?

Vivian: Generally, the accountant represents the taxpayer at the audit. Unless the IRS would expect an attorney to be involved in a certain situation, like an offshore voluntary disclosure audit, the accountant should be the face seen by the IRS. If an attorney shows up at the audit, they will think the taxpayer must have something to hide. Sometimes, clients may have done something that might not be entirely correct. In that situation, they may hire the attorney to do research in the background and help advise the accountant, while the accountant meets with the auditor. That happens from time to time. In those cases, the attorney hires the accountant to cover the accountant with the attorney-client privilege. Those types of audits are called "eggshell audits". A discussion of eggshell audits is beyond the scope of this book.

If the case goes beyond the audit phase, either an accountant or tax attorney could assist the client. Some accountants are not comfortable beyond the audit, particularly if a Tax Court Petition must be filed before going to the Appeals Division. In that case, accountants usually associate an attorney to at least file the Petition and then work with the attorney when the case goes back to Appeals.

In determining the appropriate tax attorney for the case, the business owner should consider, experience, temperament and cost. Avoid attorneys who refer to the IRS as "the evil empire" or other such nonsense. Just as the taxpayer should not antagonize the IRS, neither should his attorney. Such behavior escalates the conflict. While that is great for the attorney in billable fees, it's not great for the business owner. Find an attorney who can work with the IRS yet try a case with them in a non-antagonistic way. In that situation, the attorney and IRS counsel will work together to stipulate away all the issues except the one in which the IRS is really interested, which will reduce the cost of litigation substantially.

Business owners also need to understand law firm economics when it is time to hire a tax attorney. Traditional law firms leverage associates' time. The traditional firm operates like an Amway pyramid. The more hours billed by those under the lead attorney, the more money the attorney can make. Some big law firms have recently raised rates and lawyers right out of law school are starting at $180,000.

Jonathan: Wow.

Vivian: That kind of salary for a first-year lawyer is ridiculous. No one right out of school is worth that much, but these salaries are earned at big firms who handle the Fortune 500 companies. Those companies are paying for these lawyers to learn on the job. Unless the business is a Fortune 500 business, it should find a more reasonably priced firm. The rule could be called, "avoid marble and mahogany." It costs a lot of money and billable hours to pay for such showy overhead.

A business owner should also understand the billable hour requirements of traditional large law firms that leverage their recent law graduates. Those requirements can be anywhere from 2,000 hours to 2,100 hours per year. Think about the number of hours a lawyer would have to work to bill that many billable hours, considering the many non-billable hours of administrative work. Attorneys working in the traditional law firm model are exhausted. Does a business really want an exhausted attorney handling their tax matters?

The traditional law firm economic model of leveraging lower-tiered lawyers isn't working. Mid-tier lawyers are tired of doing all of the work to support the new lawyers and the older senior partners. They are tired of sacrificing time away from their families to bill hours that benefit other attorneys in their firms. These attorneys are rebelling and forming a new breed of law firm. A business owner should look for attorneys who have left the big firm model for quality of life and reasonable rates. These attorneys can charge lower fees because they don't pay new lawyers ridiculous wages and they don't waste money on overhead. Consequently, they can bill at more reasonable rates and concentrate on solving clients' problems.

In some firms, this is the first question the attorney asks himself: "How can I solve this person's problem for the least cost possible?" For other firms, the first thought of billable hour-hungry lawyers is this: "What is the client's net worth and how much can they pay?"

Business owners need an attorney who is interested in solving their problem even if it means only 10 hours of billable work. Nor are hourly rates a good indication of who to hire. An attorney charging $500 an hour may be able to resolve the problem in 10 hours, whereas another attorney charging $300 an hour may take two weeks. The business owner has to balance the hourly rate with the attorney's experience and the structure of the law firm.

Business owners need to interview attorneys to figure out the culture of the law firm. Find out if the firm is family oriented, and whether or not there is a strict billable hour requirement. Are the attorneys engaged in other activities like public service projects? Are the attorneys happy with their lives?

I have built my practice by word of mouth, by accountants referring work to me. Many years ago, an accountant sent me a very large case. Knowing I would have a learning curve, he still sent the case to me because he didn't like how my competitor treated one of his clients. My competitor actually said to this accountant, "If you're making money, I can keep this case going. But if you are not, we can settle it tomorrow." The accountant never sent any more business to that attorney.

Jonathan: So, you would be looking for a lawyer who not only works for your problem but also works for you?

Vivian: You are looking for a lawyer to solve your problem and provide value to you and your company not just looking to you as a one-time …

Jonathan: As a paycheck?

Vivian: Yes. Instead of seeing you as a paycheck, the attorney should be seeing you as a person. The attorney should try to solve your problem cost-effectively and treat you the way they would want to be treated if they were in the same situation. There are firms with attorneys like that. For instance, my firm doesn't have a billable hour requirement. If the attorneys don't work, they won't get paid, but maybe they need to spend time with an ailing parent or a sick child. An attorney may want to take off early because her daughter's soccer team is playing in the state championships, and that will not be held against her. That makes the work environment so much less stressful and attorneys more productive. If you can find a firm like that, hire someone there because those people will be happy in their jobs.

Jonathan: Okay.

Vivian: Most people don't understand law firm economics and they should. I successfully handled a passive loss case a few years ago for a client, and I guess he paid me the highest compliment I have ever received. He said, "Darling, it isn't the hourly rate that'll kill you but the number of hours. And based on this bill you must be the smartest damn tax attorney in town!" I should make a disclaimer here. The case did take much less time to resolve than I thought it would. And sometimes cases take more time than you think they should. It all depends on how quickly the taxpayer's lawyer and the government lawyer can have a meeting of the minds. No result is ever guaranteed. It will all depend on the specific factual and legal circumstances of the case.

I Didn't File a Tax Court Petition in Time. Is All Hope Lost?

Jonathan: Let's say I missed the deadline for filing a Tax Court Petition; so what happens now?

Vivian: There are still options for a taxpayer who failed to file a Tax Court petition, such as paying the tax and filing a refund suit in District Court. If the taxpayer cannot afford to pay the tax, then there are two other options. The taxpayer can ask for audit reconsideration, or the taxpayer can file a Doubt as to Liability Offer-in-Compromise. A second set of eyes will look at the issue and possibly reach a different conclusion, particularly if the failure to file the petition was inadvertent. A taxpayer cannot get to Tax Court through the audit reconsideration or Doubt as to Liability Offer unless she can establish that she never received the Statutory Notice of Deficiency from the IRS. In those very limited circumstances, the Court has allowed the taxpayer to litigate the underlying tax deficiency in Tax Court.

It is a complicated procedure to get a "back door" Tax Court hearing on the underlying deficiency. Yet in some of my clients' cases, even though the client missed the deadline for filing the Tax Court petition, the IRS was unable to establish that the taxpayer actually received the statutory notice so the agent(s) conceded that the underlying deficiency could be disputed in a collection-based Tax Court case. A taxpayer should never count on being able to do that, but it has happened before.

Jonathan: That almost seems like an anomaly.

Vivian: Right, but it does happen.

Employment Taxes are the Worst, Especially for Young, Rapidly Growing Businesses

Jonathan: Which area of tax gives business owners the most trouble?

Vivian: Rule number three - all returns must be filed on time. Filing and paying payroll taxes on time is the most problematic area, especially for rapidly growing businesses. Payroll comes around every week, every two weeks, or every month. The business owner has to not only make payroll but also withhold enough money from the employee's paycheck to cover the employee's required withholding tax, Social Security, and Medicare. The employer also has to pay the employer's matching portion of the Social Security and Medicare tax to the IRS. Those taxes, both the employee's share and the employer's share, have to be deposited with the IRS either monthly or semi-weekly. The employer can review IRS Publication 15 to determine which payment schedule applies to them. The employer is also required to use electronic funds transfer or payments to the Electronic Federal Tax Payment System (EFTPS) to make all Federal tax deposits. In addition, the employer has to pay all of the Federal Unemployment Tax or FUTA payment. The employer must file a Form 941 quarterly to report wages and withholdings to the IRS. The FUTA tax return, Form 940, is filed only at the end of the year.

At the same time, the business owner may have other expenses to pay in order to stay in business, such as necessary vendors.

Time and time again, even though all of their advisors instruct them not to, owners borrow these withheld trust fund amounts, that they have withheld from the employees' paychecks, to fund the business operations.

Then they make matters worse. They decide not to file the Form 941 return because they can't afford to pay the tax. Now in addition to having Failure to Deposit penalties, they have Failure to File penalties. It would be better to open and use a new line of credit to manage cash flow shortages rather than funding operations or payroll from the trust fund taxes.

To compound the problem even further, when the business owners get extra money, they try to catch up and start paying the older liabilities first even while the current liabilities are still being paid late. That is the wrong way to handle everything!

If a taxpayer gets behind in employment taxes, he needs to continue to file the Form 941 in a timely fashion for two reasons. First, the taxpayer avoids the Failure to File penalty by timely filing. Second, filing the Form 941 starts the three-year statute of limitations for personal assessment of the trust fund liability (sometimes called the "trust fund penalty") against the taxpayer.

Remember, a business owner who fails to pay over the trust fund taxes can be held personally liable for those taxes; this is also known as the "responsible party penalty". But owners are only personally liable if the IRS proposes to assess the Trust Fund penalty against them within three years of the time the return is filed. So filing the return can start that time limit running.

Unless the IRS proposes the assessment in time, the business owner cannot be held personally liable.

If the business owner has been properly assessed the trust fund liability, she can be required to pay that liability from her personal funds. Owners cannot bankrupt out of that employment tax liability, and the IRS has 10 years from the date of assessment of the tax to collect those trust fund taxes; also, interest is accruing during that entire time.

I have seen businesses get really far behind, as their owners fall further and further into debt. They will never be able to bankrupt out of these tax liabilities and they will owe those taxes personally. It's a difficult liability to manage. It's very important not to be tempted to use that money for business operations.

It is also more expensive to litigate the Responsible Party penalty than an income tax case. The Tax Court does not have jurisdiction over trust fund cases, so the taxpayer does not get to litigate the matter in Tax Court. The taxpayer has to litigate that case in District Court, which is a much more expensive venue than Tax Court.

In a trust fund case, the IRS will propose to assess the trust fund liability. The taxpayer will have 60 days to contest the liability by filing a protest with the Office of Appeals, which could agree or disagree with the taxpayer.

If Appeals disagrees, then the taxpayer has to pay the employment tax for one employee for each quarter where there is a delinquency and then file a claim for refund for each quarter on a Form 843 to get the amounts paid in for each employee for each quarter refunded to them. A trust fund tax is a divisible tax, so unlike an income tax case in which the taxpayer must pay the entire liability before filing the suit for refund in District Court, in a trust fund case the taxpayer is only required to pay a divisible portion of the tax liability which is deemed to be the tax for one employee per quarter contested.

Taxpayers make matters worse by trying to resolve the problem themselves. If they get behind in payments, they think they have to pay the older liabilities first. Meanwhile they continue to be delinquent for the current period. They are always playing catch-up unsuccessfully. That is the entirely wrong way to try to solve the problem. Rather than paying the oldest liability first, they need to concentrate on 'getting current', i.e. paying the company's current employment tax liabilities. They may have failed to pay for the first three quarters of the year, but for the fourth quarter they have to file and pay to get current. Once they are current and can stay current, they can set up an installment agreement to pay the outstanding liabilities. For some reason, taxpayers do not understand this concept even though it is very easy.

If the taxpayer is not current, the IRS will not agree to an installment agreement; the IRS will continue to levy bank accounts and garnish paychecks until the taxpayer gets current.

The IRS will stop all of these levies even if the taxpayer owes hundreds of thousands of dollars if the taxpayer will JUST GET CURRENT. Then work on a payment plan to pay the outstanding back taxes.

If a taxpayer can get and stay current, then the IRS will establish an installment agreement. Sometimes the taxpayer divides what he owes by the number of years left on the collection statute of limitations and thinks, "I can never pay off the liability in that time." That doesn't matter. As long as the taxpayer is current, it's possible to get a "partial pay installment agreement" that allows for him to pay an affordable amount for the 10 years allowed for collection. Under a Partial Pay Installment Agreement ("PPIA"), the IRS will send an agent to periodically review the taxpayer's financial circumstances. If the taxpayer's circumstances have changed for the better, the monthly installment amount may be increased. If their financial circumstances are worse, then the monthly payment may be reduced.

Jonathan: From what you're describing, taxpayers should file tax returns on time, stay current with current taxes, and get an installment agreement for the back taxes. Could an attorney or CPA help with that?

Vivian: Either an attorney or a CPA could help get the taxpayer into compliance and negotiate an installment agreement. Prior to the late '90s, there was no such thing as a PPIA; the IRS expected to collect everything during the collection period. But Congress realized that penalties and interest were accruing so that some taxpayers could never pay off the debt.

So they changed the law to allow for PPIAs, which means that every two years, the taxpayer will fill out a financial statement and the IRS and tax representative will negotiate another monthly payment amount.

This doesn't mean that the IRS will let the taxpayer keep their Maserati or the five million-dollar home with an indoor basketball court. The taxpayer will be required to live within reasonable means. The IRS website shows collection financial standards that outline basic allowances for families by area of the country. The IRS will deviate from those standards even if the taxpayer lives in a house that cost more than the allowed housing cost for the area where the taxpayer lives, if the cost of moving or the inability to sell the house impacts the taxpayer to his harm without increasing the collection potential. For the most part, families living within their means can continue to survive with some cutbacks on some luxury items. They just need to understand that the IRS will work with them. Finally, they need to be careful of these outfits that say "pay pennies on the dollar," because there's no such thing as paying pennies on the dollar.

Jonathan: Essentially, if it sounds too good to be true, it is.

Vivian: Right. Several states have gone after these outfits claiming that taxpayers can pay pennies on the dollar to solve delinquent tax debts, because the advertisements are misleading. In a few limited situations, the IRS will accept an up-front cash offer for an amount less than the debt owed.

This is known as an Offer-in-Compromise ("OIC"). But taxpayers should be advised of the eligibility requirements for obtaining an OIC of their tax liabilities because the requirements are not easy to meet. A representative should not accept payment for filing an OIC on behalf of a taxpayer when the representative knows that the taxpayer will never qualify for an OIC.

Jonathan: Let's talk about getting a lawyer; it's commonly known that people do not like lawyers. If I had to eventually hire a lawyer, how would I find one that I could trust? I know you mentioned going to a reputable law firm but that could be expensive. I will pay more for a name brand than if I pay for generic. How do I find a trustworthy lawyer whose best interests are for my issues and not for their own personal gain?

Vivian: You would talk to your accountant or regular corporate attorney and ask who they might recommend. Unfortunately, people often know their reputations but they don't know how things really, really work. It's difficult. You need to look at their resumes online and review their background. You need to ask them, "How long will this take?"

Sometimes a tax case is difficult. How long it takes depends on the government. Look for somebody who has a good track record of resolving disputes with the IRS. That's probably going to require a lot of word-of-mouth referrals, doing online research to find the right person, and interviewing those candidates to see who you feel most comfortable with – the person who you feel is looking out for your best interests. It's not easy.

Jonathan: That same process would be applied in finding a CPA as well, correct?

Vivian: That's correct. Generally, a tax attorney can help you to find a CPA that is geographically convenient for the taxpayer, but not always.

How to Handle Tax Issues and the IRS

Jonathan: If a business owner has a tax issue, what process do you take them through?

Vivian: It depends on whether the tax issue arises during an audit, or if the taxes have already been determined so we have to figure out how to pay the tax. First, I would describe each step of the process for challenging an IRS audit, and then I would explain the appeals process. Next, I would explain the differences between District Court and Tax Court, the cost effectiveness of Tax Court, and that most cases are settled in Appeals. Overall, I would say that cases can be handled cost effectively or at least much less than anticipated; all of these steps are described in this book.

Jonathan: Let's say somebody is reading the book and they want to get in touch with you to ask some questions what do they do?

Vivian: I can always be reached at my office if anyone has questions. My bio and contact information are in the back of the book. . It is always helpful if the taxpayer can explain where they are procedurally in the process. If they are not sure, then they need to provide any tax notices, revenue agent reports, and possibly, transcripts of their accounts if they have them. If the tax representative needs to order the transcripts from the IRS the taxpayer would have to provide their representative with a power of attorney.

These types of documents will quickly help the tax representative determine what the next steps in the process should be. The more information provided to their tax representative, the better.

Now Business Owners Can Handle IRS Tax Issues with More Confidence

Business owners have worked hard for everything they have. They rejected secure W-2 jobs to build a better widget or solve an unsolvable problem. They are risk takers. They create jobs and stoke the economy. They cannot risk the setbacks an IRS audit and tax challenge could cause. Tax is hard. It is not black and white. It is mostly gray and taxpayers and the IRS can disagree about what the law means and what taxpayers are allowed to do.

Getting a letter from the IRS stating they are increasing your tax liability is anyone's worst nightmare. Most business owners-- and even many accountants-- don't know where to turn for help. Now they do. When they get an IRS notice proposing to increase their tax liability they should do the following:

Step 1: Do not bury your head in the sand. Determine and calendar any deadlines and start searching for solutions immediately. Never delay.

Step 2: Upon receipt of the notice, if a CPA prepared the return, contact that CPA. Review the notice with the CPA to determine any misunderstandings or errors the IRS made when making their determinations.

Step 3: If the taxpayer's CPA cannot help, consult with a tax litigation attorney as quickly as possible and have that attorney and your CPA, if you have one, get in touch with each other. The attorney will need time to accumulate the necessary information to assist you with your defense and your CPA can help accelerate that process.

If you would like to book Vivian to speak at a conference or at a lunch and learn or some other event, please contact her at **770-541-2223** or **vhoard@taylorenglish**.com

About the Author

Vivian Hoard is a tax partner with Taylor English Duma LLP in Atlanta, GA. She solves complex tax controversy issues for both individual and business clients and has successfully represented individuals, businesses and their owners, publicly traded companies, professional athletes and their agents, entertainers, lawyers and accountants.

Ms. Hoard received her LLM in Taxation from Emory University School of Law and her JD from The University of Georgia School of Law. She is a member of the Georgia Bar and admitted to appear before the U.S. Tax Court, the U.S. District Court for the North District of Georgia, the U.S. Court of Appeals for the 11th Circuit, and U.S. Supreme Court.